Quiz &
challenges for
lovers

Do you know me well ?

This little test is designed to determine how well your spouse knows you.

You will also find a multitude of mini games and challenges that will put your couple to the test.

Good luck !

Rules of the game

Stand in front of your partner, not too far away.

Read each question without your partner being able to see them and think ahead.

Some questions will require more thought on your part, so also give your partner more time when answering them.

If he answers wrong, he is entitled to a token, otherwise you can continue the game with a kiss or hug as a reward.

This may seem like a difficult game, especially for young couples, but afterwards your partner will know a lot more about you and your bond will be even stronger.

At the end of the game, you can swap roles.

In this game there will be pledges to be given each time your partner answers wrong.

There will also be some in some challenges and mini-games.

So before you start, here are some examples of tokens that might give you some ideas.

Examples of a simple token

- Write a poem to your spouse
- Your partner chooses your next day's outfit
- Tell the truth to a question asked by your partner
- Do the dishes for a week
- No more watching your favourite show for 24 hours
- Sing the song chosen by your partner
- Do the next household task (without grumbling of course)
- Plus the right to say "no" to a certain request
- Name 3 qualities of your partner
- Prepare the next meal
- Prohibition to make a remark for 24 hours

Examples of "hot" token

- Remove an item of clothing
- Give him a three-minute massage
- Gently bite her ear sensually
- Give him four kisses in four different places
- Do an erotic dance
- Give him a hickey.
- Pour syrup on his body and lick it off.
- Your partner chooses the next position in bed
- Hold still for 1 minute. Your partner can do whatever he wants with you.
- Kiss the area that your spouse has designated for you.

 Let's go !

- Go to the store on your own and look for some food. Don't take foods that are too common (apple, banana, radish etc...) but rather things you are not used to eating.

- Once you have found your food, prepare a tasting plate for each of you (without your food being visible or recognizable by your partner) and take turns having your partner taste the food you have chosen. And of course all this blindfolded !

- If your partner doesn't guess the food you make him taste, he is entitled to a token.

What is the date of our meeting ?

Where do we meet ?

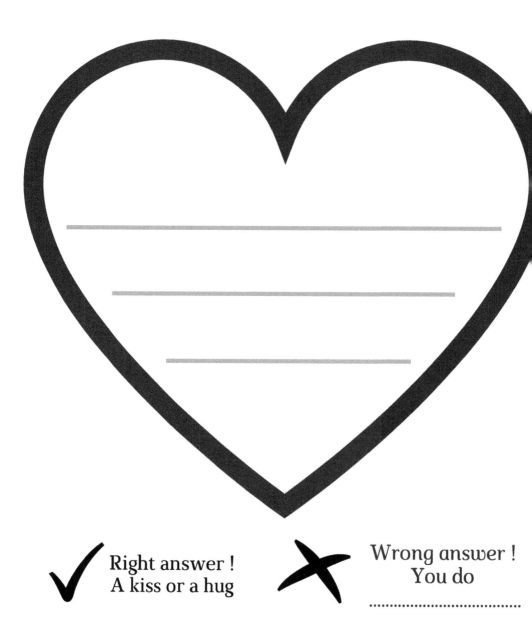

✔ Right answer !
A kiss or a hug

✗ Wrong answer !
You do

What is my favorite color ?

✓ Right answer !
A kiss or a hug

✗ Wrong answer !
You do
....

What is my favorite animal ?

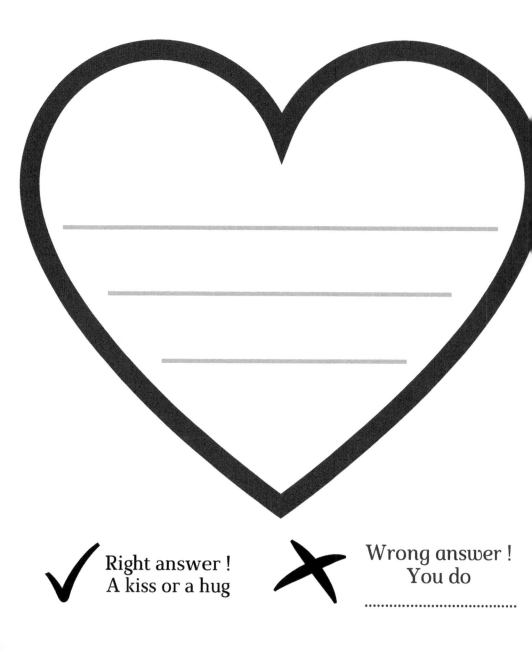

✔ Right answer !
A kiss or a hug

✗ Wrong answer !
You do

....

Your partner should turn towards the wall while you are placed right behind him/her. The aim is to make him/her guess the words you are going to write by pressing on his/her back with a thin object (or using your finger). By drawing the letters one by one, you have to spell out an action (a kiss, a hug, a massage, a ballad...) If your partner finds it, execute the action on the spot, if he doesn't find it after 3 attempts reverse the roles.

What is my greatest pride ?

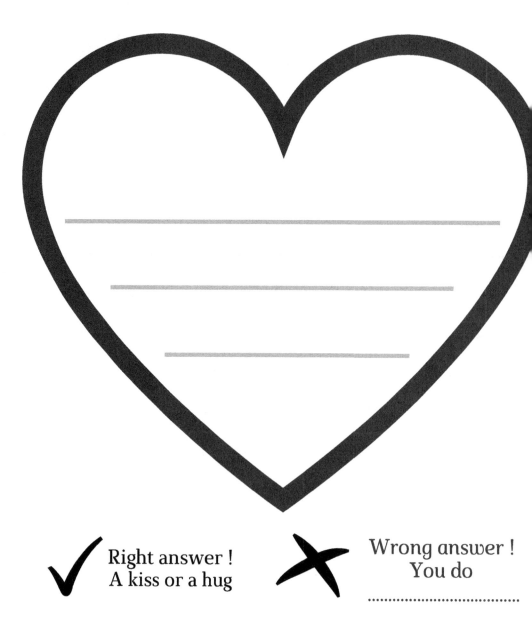

✔ Right answer !
A kiss or a hug

✘ Wrong answer !
You do
....

What is my favorite food ?

✓ Right answer !
A kiss or a hug

✗ Wrong answer !
You do
....

Who is my best friend ?

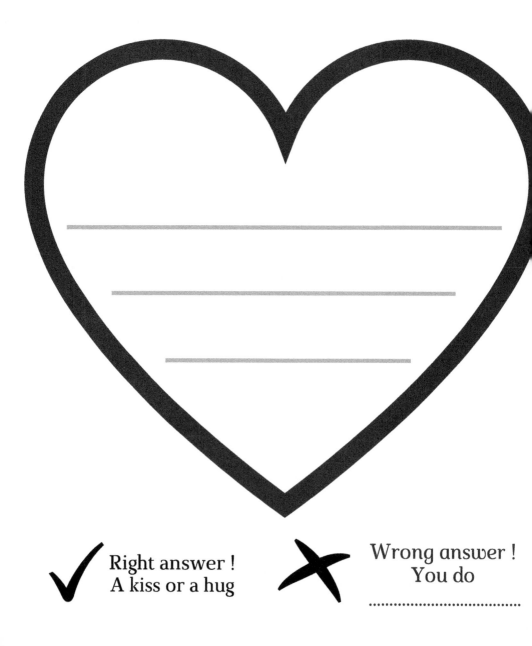

✓ Right answer !
A kiss or a hug

✗ Wrong answer !
You do
....

Did I fall directly in love with you ?

✔ Right answer !
A kiss or a hug

✗ Wrong answer !
You do
....

What part of my body do I like the least ?

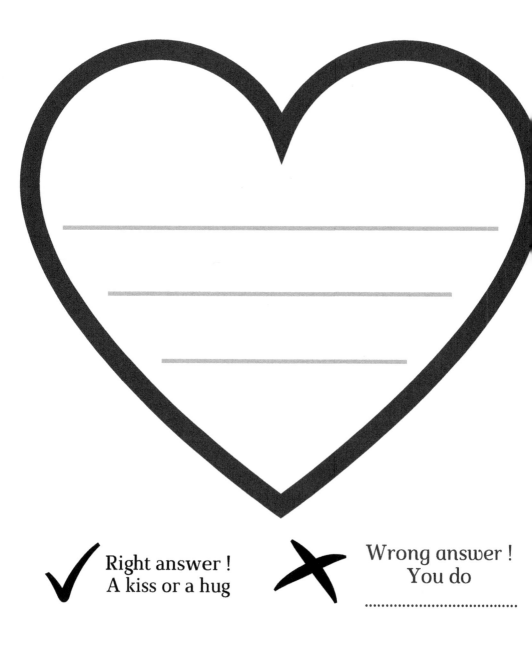

✔ Right answer !
A kiss or a hug

✗ Wrong answer !
You do
....

What is my biggest fantasy ?

Right answer !
A kiss or a hug

Wrong answer !
You do

What is my favorite dessert?

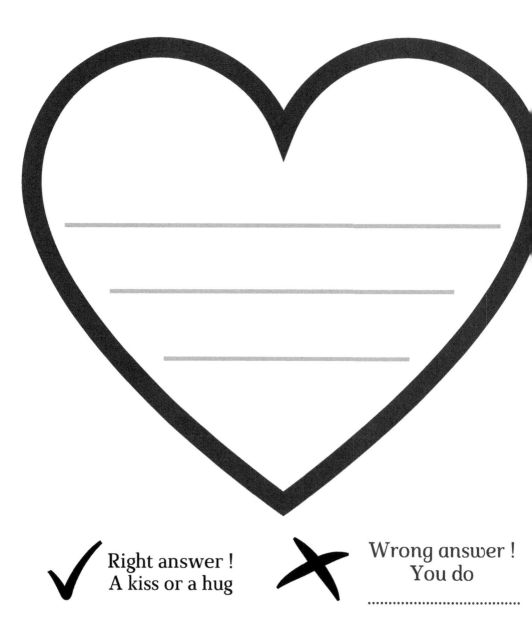

✔ Right answer !
A kiss or a hug

✗ Wrong answer !
You do
....

Who is the person I like the most among your friends ?

✔ Right answer !
A kiss or a hug

✗ Wrong answer !
You do
....

What is the first thing I look at in a person ?

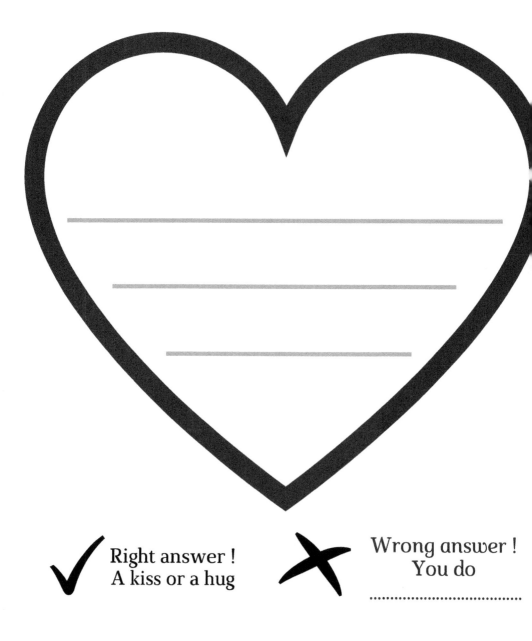

✓ Right answer !
A kiss or a hug

✗ Wrong answer !
You do
....

- Take a sheet of paper and separate it with a vertical line to create two columns. Then write 6 naughty action verbs in the first column (caress, massage, lick, kiss etc...). Then write in the other column 6 parts of the body (buttocks, ears, lower back, belly etc...).
- One of you starts and throws a dice, twice. You will then have to perform the action on the part of the body that the dice will have designated.
- Example: the first die rolled falls on a 4 and designates the action "kiss" in the first column. The second die is a 6 and designates the "lower back" body part in the second column. The player will then have to kiss his partner's lower back.

What was the best day of my life ?

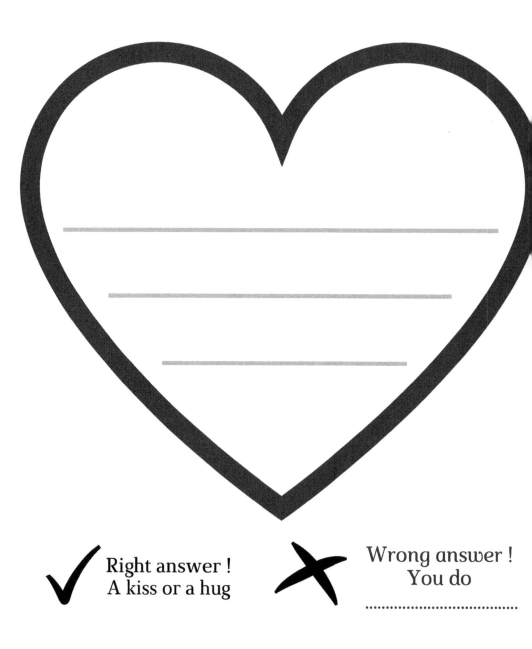

✔ Right answer !
A kiss or a hug

✗ Wrong answer !
You do

....

What is my dream weekend ?

✔ Right answer !
A kiss or a hug

✗ Wrong answer !
You do
....

In which country(ies) have I travelled before ?

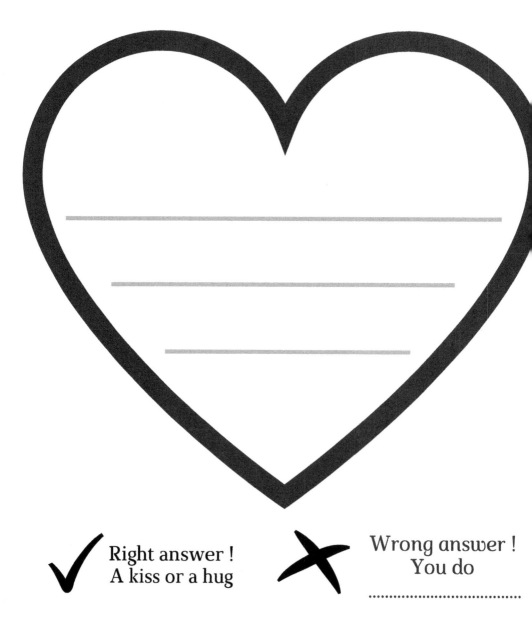

✓ Right answer !
A kiss or a hug

✗ Wrong answer !
You do
....

What was my nickname as a kid ?

✓ Right answer !
A kiss or a hug

✗ Wrong answer !
You do
....

Challenge !

For this challenge you will need a headset (or headphones). One of you must put the headphones on while the music is playing. He or she must not be able to hear anything other than the music. The other must then whisper a few words or a small sentence, trying to articulate well (small soft words allowed). The player with the headphones must guess the words spoken by trying to read his lips. The first one of you who manages to decipher what his partner is saying wins this challenge and has to give a token to the other one.

What was my first vehicle ?

✔ **Right answer !**
A kiss or a hug

✗ **Wrong answer !**
You do
....

Where was I born ?

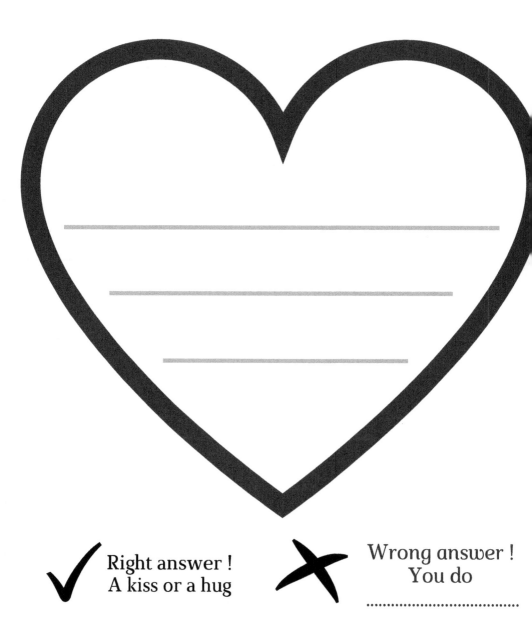

✔ Right answer !
A kiss or a hug

✗ Wrong answer !
You do
....

What's my date of birth ?

✓ Right answer !
A kiss or a hug

✗ Wrong answer !
You do
....

How many times a week do I work out ?

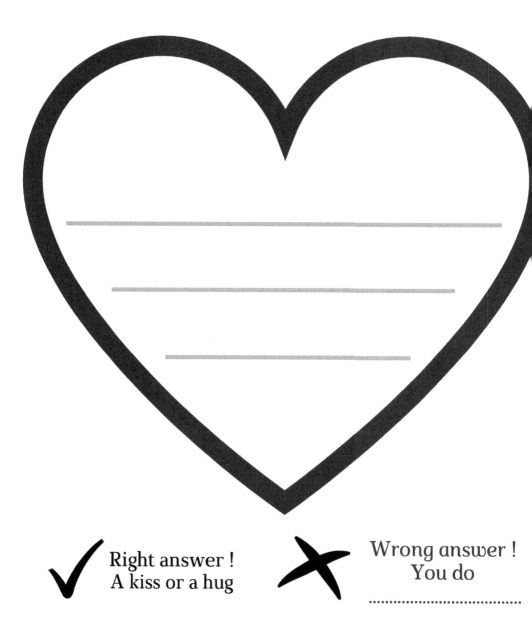

✓ Right answer !
A kiss or a hug

✗ Wrong answer !
You do
....

Was the job I was doing the job I wanted to do ?

✔ Right answer !
A kiss or a hug

✗ Wrong answer !
You do
....

What is my level in cooking ?

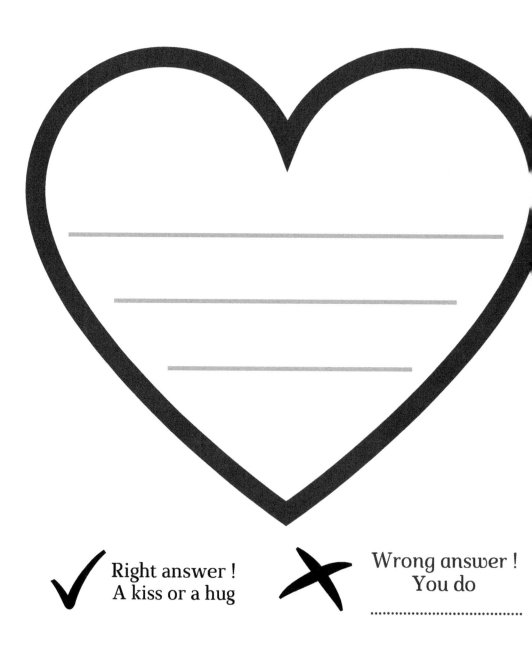

✓ Right answer !
A kiss or a hug

✗ Wrong answer !
You do
....

Have I always lived in the same country ?

✓ **Right answer !**
A kiss or a hug

✗ Wrong answer !
You do
....

What is the ideal number of children in my opinion ?

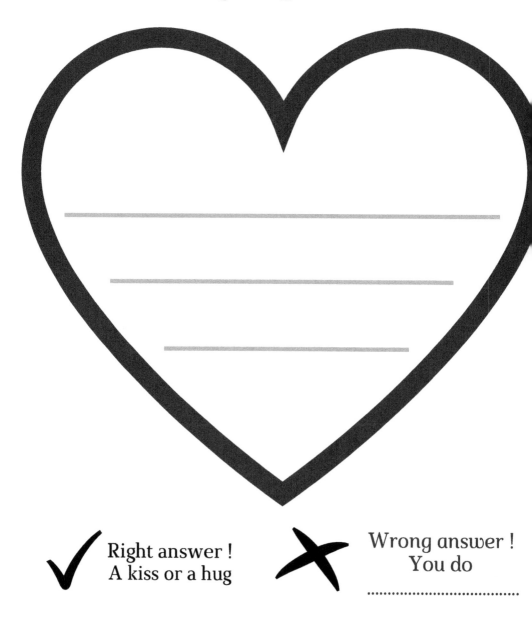

✔ Right answer ! A kiss or a hug

✗ Wrong answer ! You do

....

What is the ideal number of children in my opinion ?

✔ Right answer !
A kiss or a hug

✗ Wrong answer !
You do
....

- Write 5 activities each on 5 small pieces of paper. These can be a romantic walk, play a board game, watch your favourite movie, go back to your meeting place, take a shower together, take an intimate position... Anything that can please both of you!
- Then put the little pieces of paper in an empty jar and mix them together. As the evening progresses, pick up the small pieces of paper and carry out the activity indicated on the spot.
- If the action cannot be done right away, postpone it until the next day.

What is my middle name ?

✓ Right answer !
A kiss or a hug

✗ Wrong answer !
You do
....

What is my biggest dream ?

✓ **Right answer !**
A kiss or a hug

✗ **Wrong answer !**
You do

Have I ever been in the newspaper ?

✓ Right answer !
A kiss or a hug

✗ Wrong answer !
You do
....

Do I believe in the paranormal ?

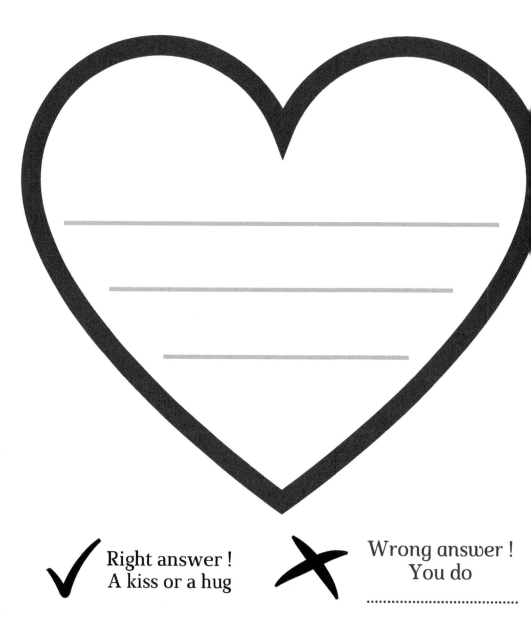

✓ Right answer !
A kiss or a hug

✗ Wrong answer !
You do
....

Challenge !

You set a certain amount and you have a week to find a nice and original gift to give to the other person with this amount !

What is my level of education ?

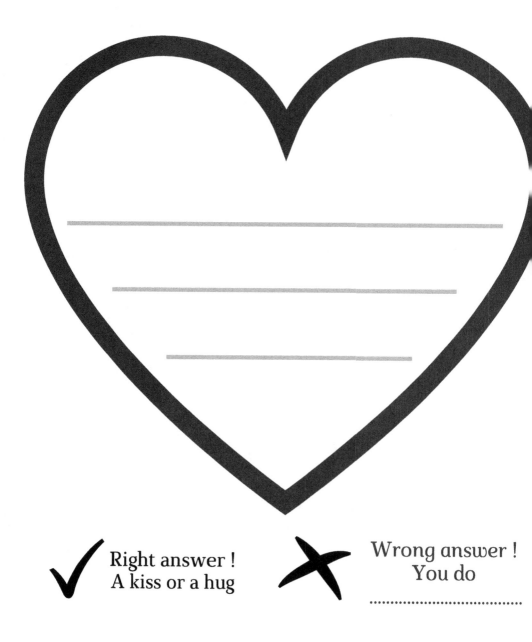

✓ Right answer !
A kiss or a hug

✗ Wrong answer !
You do
....

Am I a greedy person ?

✓ Right answer !
A kiss or a hug

✗ Wrong answer !
You do
....

What is my favourite clothing brand ?

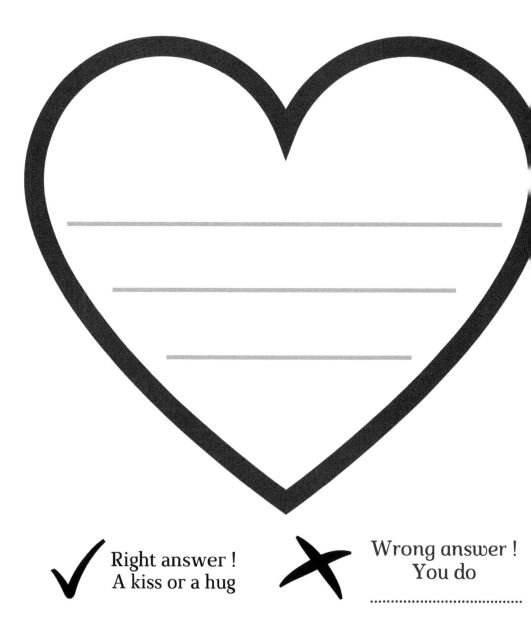

Right answer !
A kiss or a hug

Wrong answer !
You do
....

What is my biggest flaw ?
(be careful)

✓ Right answer !
A kiss or a hug

✗ Wrong answer !
You do
....

What was my longest relationship ?

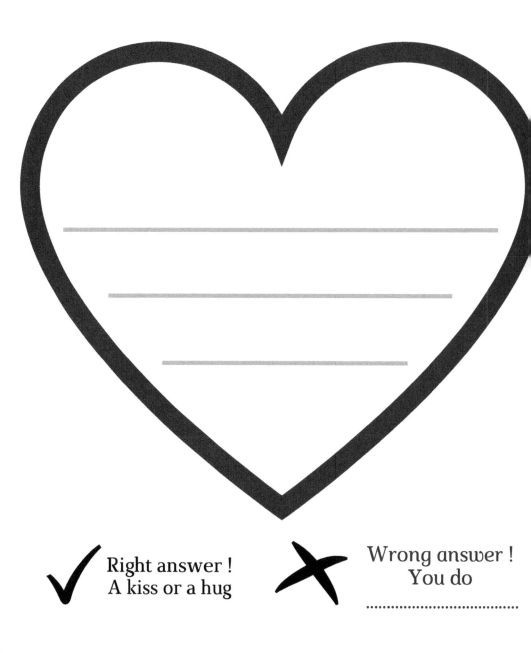

✔ Right answer !
A kiss or a hug

✗ Wrong answer !
You do
....

How do I express my anger ?

✓ Right answer !
A kiss or a hug

✗ Wrong answer !
You do

....

What do I need to relax ?

Right answer !
A kiss or a hug

Wrong answer !
You do

What kind of person can't stand me ?

✓ **Right answer !**
A kiss or a hug

✗ Wrong answer !
You do
....

I prefer to be oppressed or abandoned ?

✓ Right answer !
A kiss or a hug

✗ Wrong answer !
You do

- The object of the game will be to place yourself behind your partner at any time of the day in order to act in his place. As if you were 2 in 1 !
- Preparing a meal, showering, washing dishes, doing your hair, shaving, eating, drinking, reading, paying for groceries at the supermarket, buying a subway ticket, etc...
- Each activity is an opportunity to surprise your partner. Doing it in public can also be a lot of fun !

What pisses me off more than anything else ?

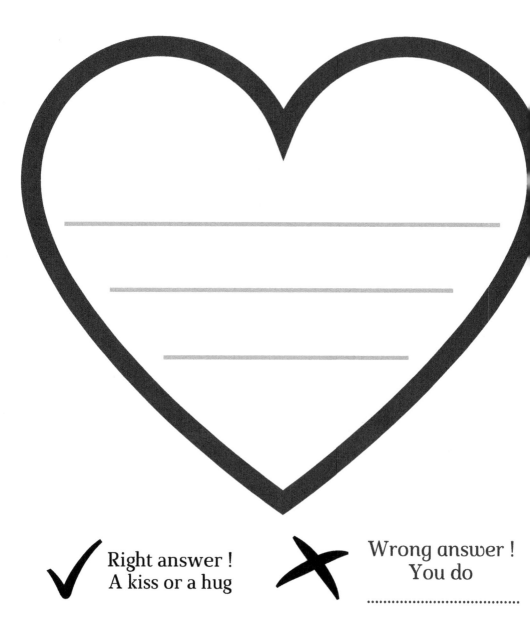

✓ Right answer !
A kiss or a hug

✗ Wrong answer !
You do
....

Am I dependent on my family ?

✓ Right answer !
A kiss or a hug

✗ Wrong answer !
You do
....

Do I prefer TV or reading ?

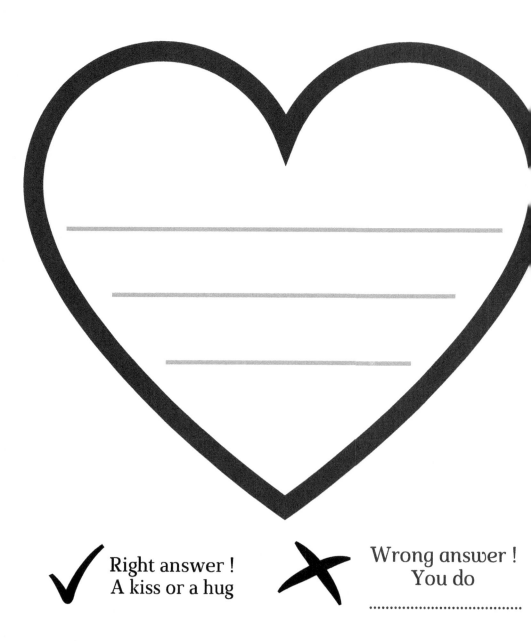

✓ Right answer !
A kiss or a hug

✗ Wrong answer !
You do

What's my relationship to money?

✓ Right answer !
A kiss or a hug

✗ Wrong answer !
You do
....

Challenge !

You've been invited to a dinner party and you don't feel like being bored ? Then prepare a list of 10 words that are difficult to place in a conversation, such as "puzzle", "interview" or "homophone". Just before you go to dinner, give each of you your list to your partner. The goal will be to place as many words as possible without being noticed ! The winner has the right to give a token to the loser once the evening is over.

If I won a million euros tomorrow, what would I do ?

✓ Right answer !
A kiss or a hug

✗ Wrong answer !
You do
....

How do I imagine the perfect life ?

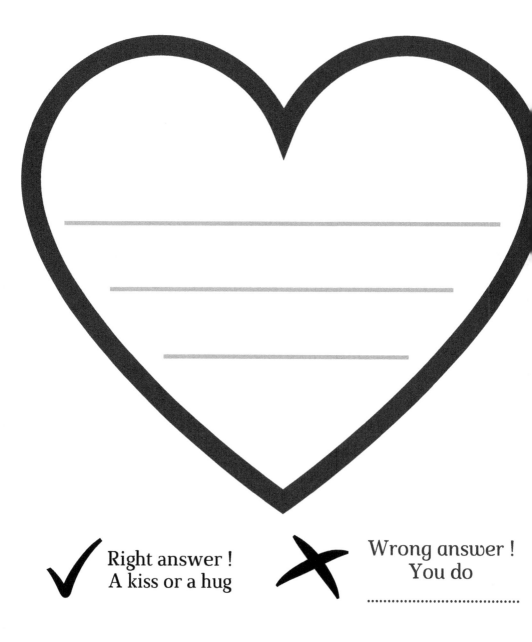

✓ Right answer !
A kiss or a hug

✗ Wrong answer !
You do
....

Did I like (primary) school when I was small ?

_____

_____

_____

✓ Right answer !
A kiss or a hug

✗ Wrong answer !
You do
....

I prefer to spend my life travelling or building a stable home ?

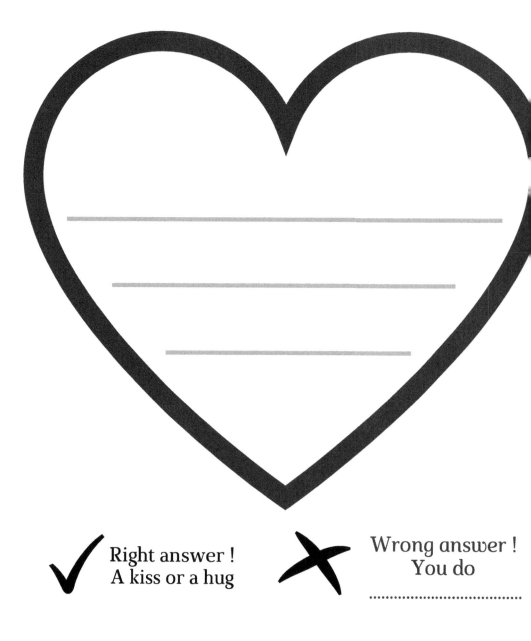

✓ Right answer !
A kiss or a hug

✗ Wrong answer !
You do
....

If I could meet a famous person (dead or alive), which one would I choose ?

✓ Right answer !
A kiss or a hug

✗ Wrong answer !
You do
....

What's my maternal last name ?

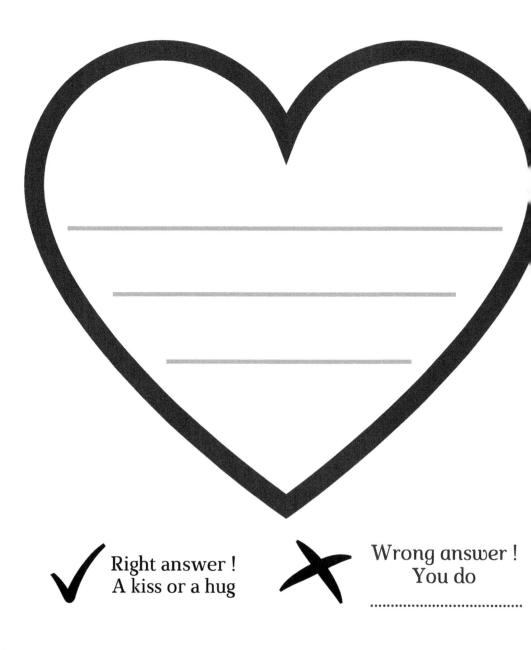

✔ Right answer !
A kiss or a hug

✗ Wrong answer !
You do
....

If I ruled the world, what would I change first ?

✔ **Right answer !**
A kiss or a hug

✗ **Wrong answer !**
You do
....

What's my greatest talent ?

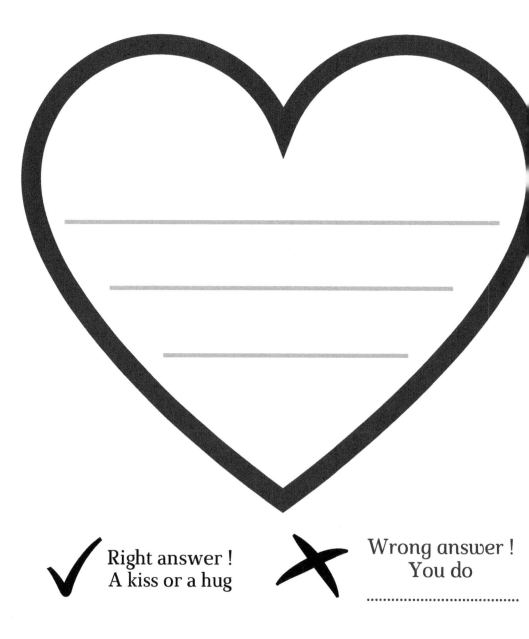

✔ Right answer !
A kiss or a hug

✗ Wrong answer !
You do

....

What is my favorite kind of chocolate ?

_____

_____

_____

✓ **Right answer !**
A kiss or a hug

✗ **Wrong answer !**
You do
....

- Everybody knows it's nicer to kiss with your eyes closed. In this minigame you will do it without any other possibility!
- You both have to blindfold each other and place yourself in a large room (or even outside if possible). The goal will be to find you only by your hearing and kiss you (it's forbidden to use your hands and remove the blindfold).
- You may think it's easy, but you'll see that it's not! Especially if there are obstacles in your way. Anyway love is blind so you'll end up finding each other again.
- PS: It can be fun if you decide to film yourself, so you can see afterwards how hard you've struggled to find yourself.

Am I allergic ? If yes, to what ?

✓ Right answer !
A kiss or a hug

✗ Wrong answer !
You do

....

Do I speak another language ?

Right answer !
A kiss or a hug

Wrong answer !
You do

....

What is my favorite smell ?

✓ Right answer !
A kiss or a hug

✗ Wrong answer !
You do
....

Do I prefer dogs or cats ?

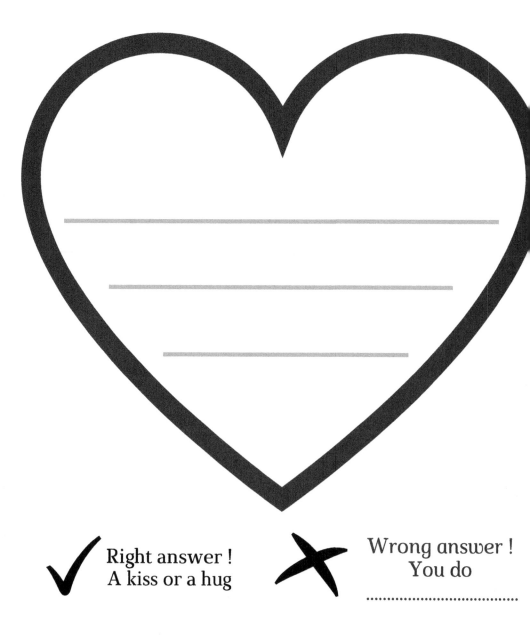

✔ Right answer !
A kiss or a hug

✗ Wrong answer !
You do
....

Each choose 2 unrelated foods, e.g. strawberries with ginger, coffee with banana, peanuts with apricots... Your goal is to invent an original and enjoyable recipe. Whoever finds the best combination will win the challenge and give a prize to the loser !

Do I prefer the city or the country ?

✔ Right answer !
A kiss or a hug

✗ Wrong answer !
You do
....

Which city(ies) would I like to visit ?

✔ **Right answer !**
A kiss or a hug

✗ **Wrong answer !**
You do
....

What is my biggest regret ?

✓ Right answer !
A kiss or a hug

✗ Wrong answer !
You do
....

Would I rather be rich or famous ?

✔ **Right answer !**
A kiss or a hug

✗ **Wrong answer !**
You do
....

What is my favorite movie ?

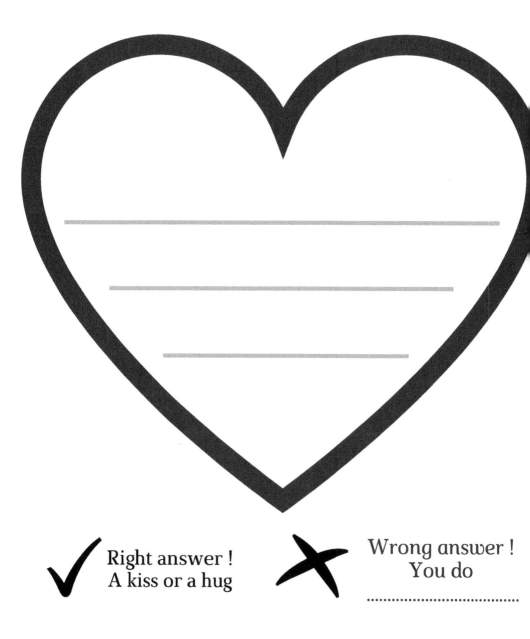

✓ Right answer !
A kiss or a hug

✗ Wrong answer !
You do
....

Who is my favorite singer ?

✓ Right answer !
A kiss or a hug

✗ Wrong answer !
You do
....

What is my favorite song ?

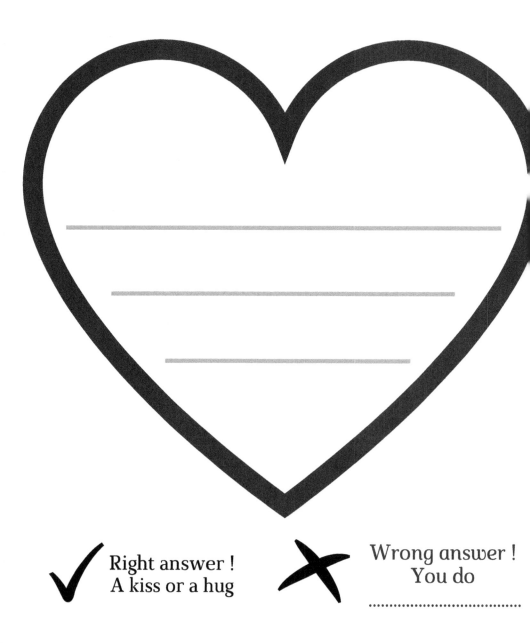

✓ Right answer !
A kiss or a hug

✗ Wrong answer !
You do
....

What language would I like to learn ?

✓ **Right answer !**
A kiss or a hug

✗ Wrong answer !
You do

....

What is my worst memory ?

✔ Right answer !
A kiss or a hug

✗ Wrong answer !
You do
....

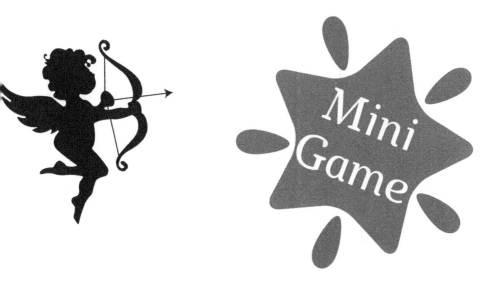

- Go to the store or directly online and buy a small notebook. Your goal will be to write down all the important things you've done since the beginning of your relationship.
- Sometimes you'll find that something that was important to you may not necessarily be important to your partner and vice versa.
- You don't have to write it all down at once, doing it a few times before you go to bed can be a good idea and can spark some great topics for discussion !

What is my fondest memory ?

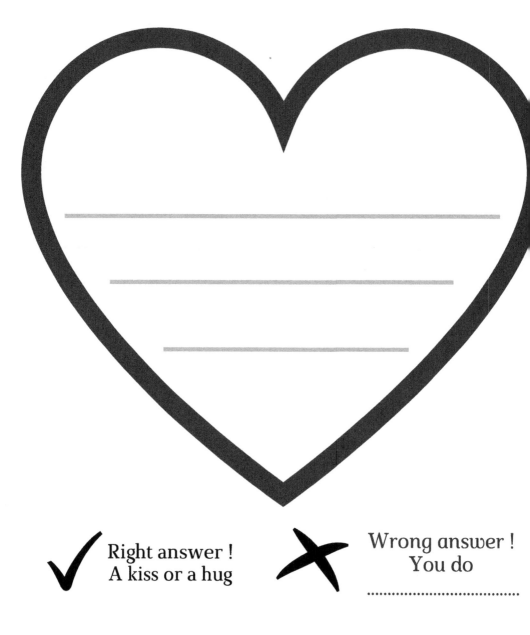

✔ Right answer !
A kiss or a hug

✗ Wrong answer !
You do
....

What is my relationship with my mother ?

_____

_____

_____

✔ Right answer !
A kiss or a hug

✘ Wrong answer !
You do
....

What was our first discussion ?

✓ Right answer !
A kiss or a hug

✗ Wrong answer !
You do
....

What is the craziest thing I've ever done in my life ?

✓ Right answer !
A kiss or a hug

✗ Wrong answer !
You do
....

Challenge !

The winner of the last mini-game has to lie on his stomach and close his eyes. The loser massages the winner with part of his body. The winner must then try to guess what the masseur is using to massage him. If he fails to guess after 3 attempts, reverse the roles. If you want to complicate the game after several massages, you can use objects. You will be surprised how pleasant some objects are for massaging.

When was the last time I lied ?

✓ Right answer !
A kiss or a hug

✗ Wrong answer !
You do
....

What was the name of my first pet ?

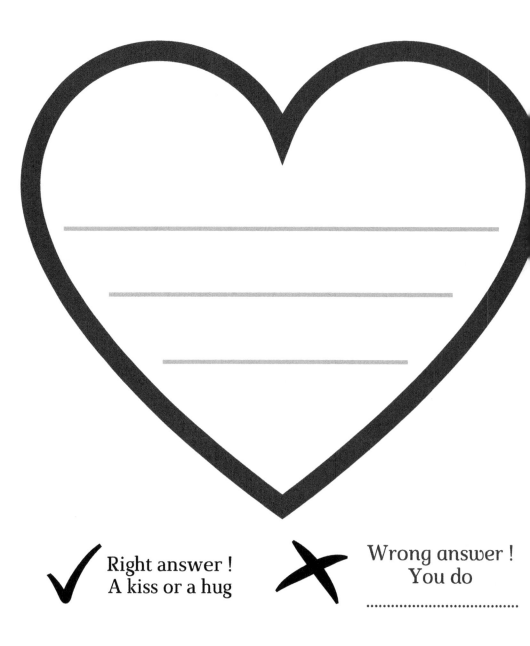

✔ **Right answer !**
A kiss or a hug

✘ Wrong answer !
You do
....

What have I ever done that I'll never do again ?

✔ Right answer !
A kiss or a hug

✗ Wrong answer !
You do
....

Have I ever stolen anything ?

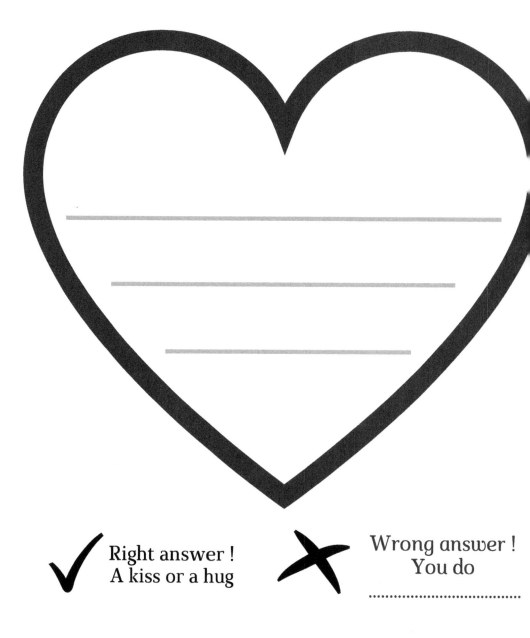

✓ Right answer !
A kiss or a hug

✗ Wrong answer !
You do

What am I afraid of ?

✓ Right answer !
A kiss or a hug

✗ Wrong answer !
You do
....

Do I look more like my mom or dad ?

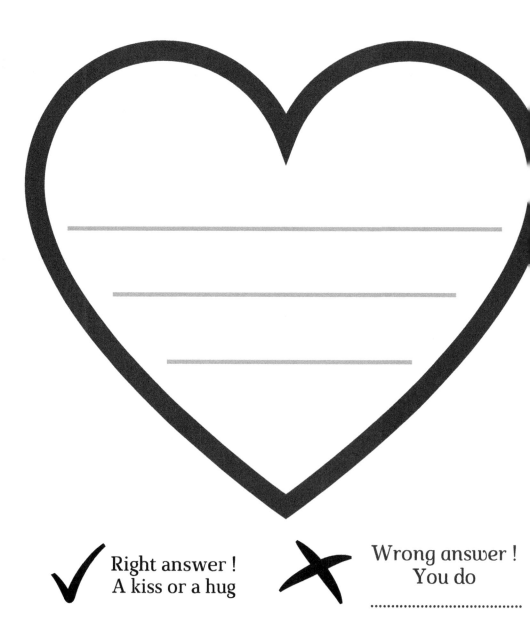

✓ Right answer !
A kiss or a hug

✗ Wrong answer !
You do

Am I usually the jealous type ?

✓ **Right answer !**
A kiss or a hug

✗ **Wrong answer !**
You do
....

Have I ever tried drugs ?

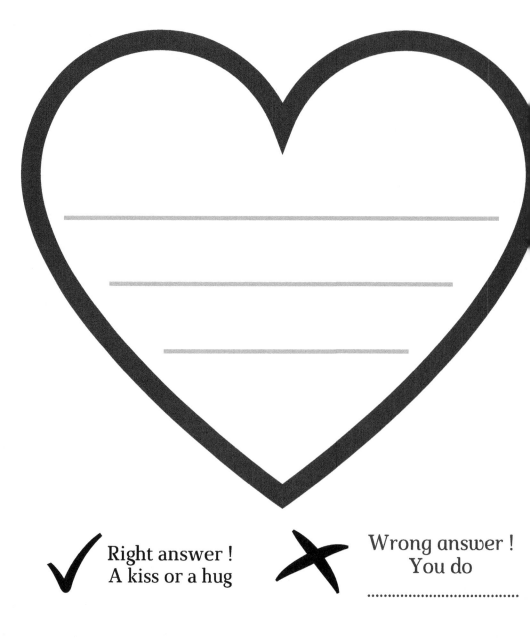

✓ **Right answer !**
A kiss or a hug

✗ **Wrong answer !**
You do

....

Who is my favourite actor (or actress) ?

✔ Right answer !
A kiss or a hug

✗ Wrong answer !
You do
....

- At the beginning of the day, work out a list of about 15 words with your partner. Not too common and not too rare. Here are a few examples: I like, restaurant, ball, perfume, bottle, shoe, music, light, etc...
- As the day progresses, if you hear any of the words on the list, you should kiss each other. Whether you are at the movies, at a party with friends, or at home watching a movie, you must kiss on the spot without saying anything.
- If one of you has heard the word but the other one has forgotten the game, nothing better than a token to remind them of the rules !

Am I photogenic ?

Right answer !
A kiss or a hug

Wrong answer !
You do
....

Do I like spending time on social networks ?

✓ Right answer !
A kiss or a hug

✗ Wrong answer !
You do

Do I like to play video games ?

✓ Right answer !
A kiss or a hug

✗ Wrong answer !
You do
....

Do I like rain ?

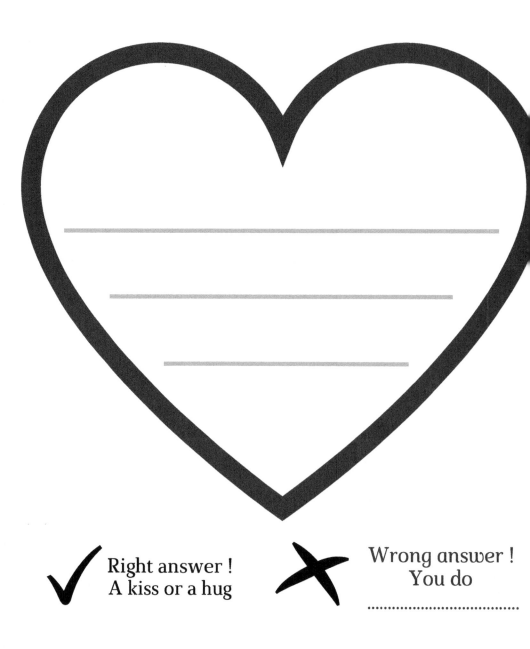

✔ Right answer !
A kiss or a hug

✗ Wrong answer !
You do
....

For tonight's meal choose one character each, e.g. nurse, policeman, bandit etc... The goal will be to play a character during the whole evening, in a sexy version of course. If it's too late to do this challenge, postpone it to the next day.

Do I prefer sweet or salty ?

✓ Right answer !
A kiss or a hug

✗ Wrong answer !
You do
....

Am I said to be stingy or generous ?

✓ Right answer !
A kiss or a hug

✗ Wrong answer !
You do
....

Am I afraid to get on a plane ?

✓ Right answer !
A kiss or a hug

✗ Wrong answer !
You do

What is the biggest mistake I made as a kid?

✓ **Right answer !**
A kiss or a hug

✗ Wrong answer !
You do
....

- Sit or stand opposite each other and look into each other's eyes.
- The goal is to hold on as long as possible without blinking, laughing or moving. Wincing is allowed!
- The first of you to break the rule has a token from the winner.

What was my dream job when I was a kid ?

✔ Right answer !
A kiss or a hug

✘ Wrong answer !
You do
....

What's my favorite show ?

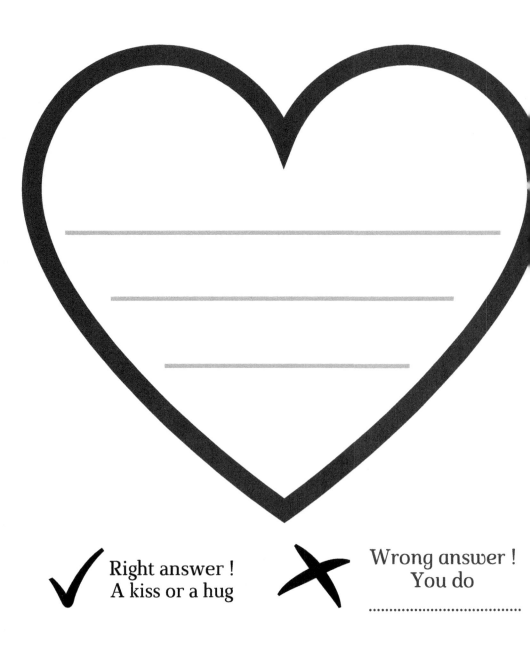

✓ Right answer !
A kiss or a hug

✗ Wrong answer !
You do
....

Do I prefer to be conspicuous or discreet ?

Right answer !
A kiss or a hug

Wrong answer !
You do

Have I ever picked something up from the fridge while you were asleep ?

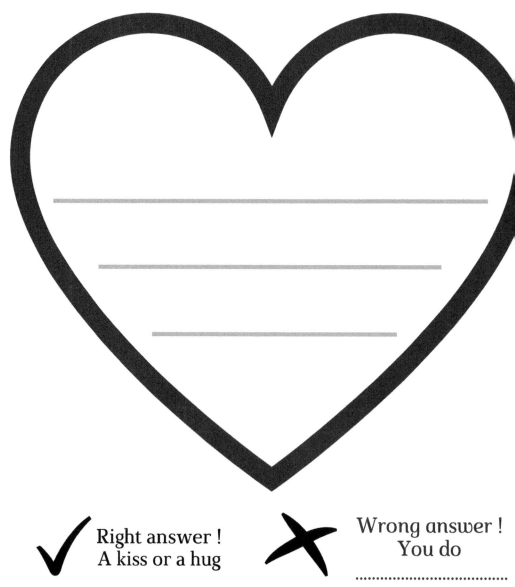

✓ Right answer !
A kiss or a hug

✗ Wrong answer !
You do
....

Take a small ball and a salad bowl. Put the bowl on the floor and sit down on one side, leaving enough space so that the game is not too easy. If possible, sit on a mat for extra comfort. Once you have settled down, take turns throwing the ball into the bowl. Each time one of you misses the bowl, you have to take off an item of clothing! The game ends when one of the two players is completely naked.

What is my zodiac sign ?

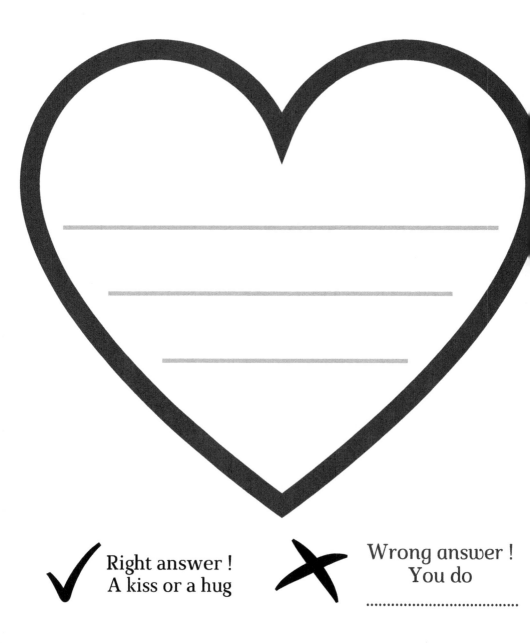

✔ Right answer !
A kiss or a hug

✗ Wrong answer !
You do

....

Do I prefer the heat or the cool ?

✓ **Right answer !**
A kiss or a hug

✗ **Wrong answer !**
You do
....

Do I believe in alien life ?

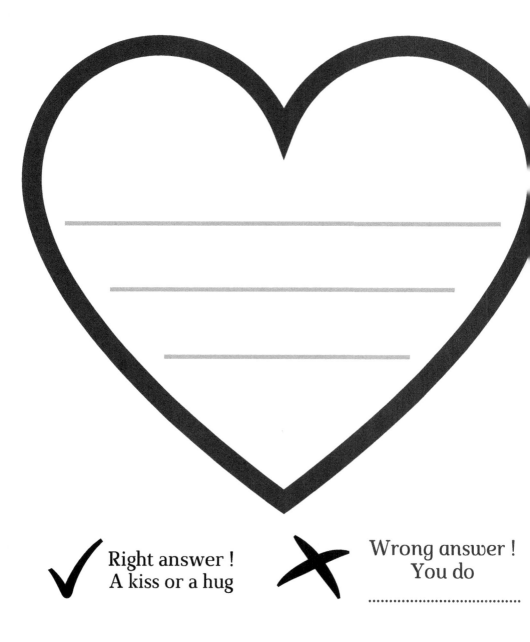

Right answer !
A kiss or a hug

Wrong answer !
You do

How many times have I moved since I was born ?

✓ Right answer !
A kiss or a hug

✗ Wrong answer !
You do
....

Do I prefer the sea or the mountains ?

✔ Right answer !
A kiss or a hug

✗ Wrong answer !
You do
....

If I could change anything in our relationship, what would it be ?

✔ Right answer !
A kiss or a hug

✗ Wrong answer !
You do
....

How old was I when I got my first smartphone ?

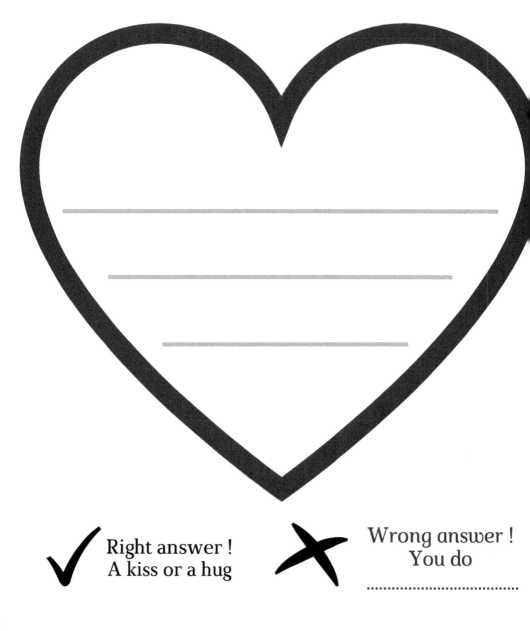

✔ **Right answer !**
A kiss or a hug

✗ **Wrong answer !**
You do
....

What's my favorite band ?

✓ **Right answer !**
A kiss or a hug

✗ **Wrong answer !**
You do
....

What is the part of my body that I love the most ?

Right answer !
A kiss or a hug

Wrong answer !
You do
....

Do you think I lied when I played that test ?

✓ **Right answer !**
A kiss or a hug

✗ Wrong answer !
You do
....

Printed in Great Britain
by Amazon